CAMERA CONFIDENCE: MASTERING AND MARKETING CONTENT CREATION

The Beginners Guide to Gaining Camera Confidence and Making Money as a Video Influencer

MOHHAN EESHAT

TABLE OF CONTENTS

INTRODUCTION

Step into the exciting world of 'Camera Confidence: Mastering and Marketing Content Creation,' where we are about to unleash the secrets to making your content truly shine! This book is like your cool, content-creating buddy, perfect for upcoming Content Creators, YouTubers, TikTokers, Live Streamers and so on. Ready to transform your videos from 'meh' to 'wow'?

Get ready for an adventure in marketing and monetizing your creations – we've got the inside scoop on turning your passion into a real moneymaker. Dive into the world of promoting your content like a pro across social media, and watch your followers skyrocket!

But wait, there's more! Flip through the pages for awesome tips and creative ideas on what to post. From viral challenges to storytelling magic, we've got your back. Learn the secrets of viewer engagement and become a content creator that everyone can't get enough of!

And that's not all – 'Camera Confidence' isn't just about the numbers. It's your guide to turning followers into a friendly, loyal community. Build those real connections that make your audience eagerly await every upload.

So, whether you're just starting out or looking to level up your content game, 'Camera Confidence' is your go-to friendly handbook for conquering the digital realm. Let's turn your passion into a captivating journey that everyone will want to be a part of – because creating awesome content should be as fun as it sounds!"

Why Content Creation Matters

Let's kick things off with the burning question: Why does content creation matter? Imagine this: you're scrolling through your favorite social media platform, and suddenly, a video grabs your attention. It's not just any video; it's one that makes you laugh, think, or maybe even shed a tear. That, my friend, is the magic of content creation.

It's not just about posting stuff online; it's about crafting experiences, sparking conversations, and building connections. Whether you're a seasoned creator or just starting, understanding the importance of what you're putting out there lays the groundwork for your creative journey.

And here's the bonus—content creation isn't just about sharing your story; it can also be your ticket to earning some moolah online. Yup, you heard it right. We're talking about turning your passion into a paycheck, and we'll definitely get into the nitty-gritty of that as we explore this exciting world. To effectively market your content, it's essential to understand your target audience.

In this book, "Camera Confidence: Mastering and Marketing Content Creation," we explore steps on Epic Content, Epic Marketing: The Dynamic Duo are unleashed. The Power of Effective Marketing Strategies, the basic ways to boost your camera confidence, A great variety of methods to fuel your creativity, A reliable plan to ensure you have a real presence online and Simple Strategies for high reach and visibility.

CHAPTER 1: AUDIENCE

Understanding Your Audience

In Coastal Naples, Italy, there once lived a chef by the name of Di Natalie in 1890's. He enjoyed playing around with flavors and coming up with unusual recipes. One day, he decided to open his own restaurant. To ensure their menu would be a hit, Di Natalie went around town, asking people about their favorite foods and what they enjoyed most about dining out. Armed with this valuable insight, He crafted a menu that catered to the tastes and preferences of their future customers.

The restaurant quickly became a local favorite, with people flocking in to savor the delicious and personalized dishes. Natalie's story reminds us of the power of understanding our audience and catering to their desires.

The idea behind content marketing is still the same in the modern era. Before you start creating, as a content creator, you must identify who your audience is.

Who do they represent? What are their desires?

What would trigger their curiosity?

How does your offering address their issues?

You may create more interesting and intriguing content by providing answers to these questions. In this chapter, we're diving deep into the art of understanding your audience— the magical key to crafting content that not only speaks but sings to the hearts of your viewers.

What is an Audience?

An audience of content creators refers to the people who consume and engage with the content that creators produce. They can be viewers, readers, or listeners who enjoy and interact with the content in various ways.

As you gather information on your audience, keep the following in mind:

Geographic Information:

The targeted region is this. It could be a particular nation, state, or city. The other two components would be more particular if your target geographic area was the entire planet. A content creator situated in New Orleans, Louisiana, might, for instance, create videos that highlight the city's exciting music scene, mouthwatering food, and colorful culture. They could go over regional celebrations like Mardi Gras, point out famous sites like the French Quarter, or tell tales that encapsulate New Orleans culture. By emphasizing regional content, producers can connect with an audience that values and identifies with the distinctive features of a particular state or city.

Demographic Information:

Data related to age, gender, place of residence, income, and education are all considered demographics. This information is essential when because it allows you to target the right people. For instance, a YouTuber who creates content for teenagers might focus on topics and trends that are relevant to that demographic, while a blogger who writes about traditional recipes might target a specific cultural group. By considering the demographics of their audience, content creators can create content that resonates with and appeals to their target audience.

Psychographic Information:

Comparatively speaking to the first two components, psychographic information is far less clear. It speaks to the character attributes and way of life that your potential clients identify with. This is arguably the most crucial component of a target audience, according to many.

This is where you get into the weeds of target audience research with habits, behavioral nuances, interests, motivations, hobbies, favorite celebrities (influencers), and so on. Stated differently, the core of psychographics lies in having a profound personal understanding of your target audience and how they engage with your material.

Stay focused as we set out to discover the techniques for engaging your audience like a digital whisperer.

Identifying Your Target Audience

Alright, let's start with the basics. Who are you creating for? Your mom, your neighbor's cat, or maybe the intergalactic community? Nah, probably not the last one. Identifying your target audience is like picking your dream team. You want people who resonate with your vibe, get your humor, and nod enthusiastically at your wisdom.

When creating a target audience, presuming you can reach EVERYONE is maybe the worst error you can make. A very little number of business can pull this off with any degree of success. When I say "very few," I mean companies like Apple, Amazon, Google, and so on. Most brands need to have a specific target audience hammered out for their content strategy.

Think about it—when you know who you're talking to, creating content becomes a breeze. It's like having a chat with a friend who just "gets" you. We'll get into creating audience personas, those imaginary friends who represent your ideal viewers. By understanding their quirks, preferences, and digital hangout spots, you'll be one step closer to content creation wizardry.

And hey, identifying your audience isn't just about demographics; it's about vibes and interests. Imagine you're hosting the ultimate party—knowing your audience is like curating the perfect guest list.

Identifying your target audience is the first step in creating content that will resonate with them. It can be difficult, but it's necessary to produce successful and useful material!

This is a collection of our finest advice, which includes analyzing your target audience's age, interests, ambitions, and demographics as well as what content appeals to them the most you identify who your target audience is:

1. Look at your existing audience

When you already have a following, you can use this to your advantage by taking the time to do some much-needed research! Who are they? What age group do they fall into? What do they find interesting?

You can also look into the demographics of your current audience – location, income level, employment, and more. With this data, you may gain a deeper understanding of your audience's characteristics, interests, and motivations for engaging with your content.

Remember that as a digital creator, your work only exists – quite literally – digitally. This means that most of your audience may come from online sources, such as social media! As a result, it's critical to consider your current following as well as the likes and views on each particular post.

2. Research your niche

Begin by researching creators in the niche you want to enter. Take a look at the kinds of content they produce and the reactions their followers receive.

Look for patterns between the responses of different target audiences and develop a profile for them. This will assist you in producing material that appeals to each distinct audience and increases the likelihood that they will interact with your work.

3. Understand your competitors

Who is your competition? Take a look at their target audiences and the content they are producing. You'll have a clearer idea of who to target with your content after reading this. Along with learning how to stand out from the competition, you can also learn what kinds of material can be popular.

4. Experiment with different types of content

You ought to try out other content kinds as well. There are several ways to connect with and engage your target audience, ranging from quick videos to infographics and podcasts.

It's crucial to experiment with several forms to see which ones suit you the best. This will assist you in determining the kinds of material that appeal to your target audience as well as the most engaging pieces.

After you've determined what kinds of material your audience like, you can utilize that knowledge to produce future content that is both more engaging and effective.

5. Identify your goals and core values

It's critical to ascertain your own objectives and guiding principles in addition to knowing your audience. With your content, what goals do you hope to achieve? Who are you as a creator?

You may produce more targeted content that can be adjusted for various audiences by using these questions.

Having well-defined objectives and guiding principles will make it simpler to assess the effectiveness of your material and make any adjustments.

6. Monitor and optimize content

Lastly, monitor the effectiveness of your material to see which sections are effective and modify as necessary. In addition to knowing what part of content creation to focus on, you will also be able to identify potential problems or areas for improvement, which allow you to adjust your content and maximize its performance.

You may produce successful content by researching your competition, optimizing your material, and keeping abreast of the most recent statistics and trends. To make sure that your content speaks to the people you want to reach, try utilizing the above-mentioned advice.

Creating Content for Different Platforms

Now, let's talk platforms—those bustling digital neighborhoods where your content can set up shop. Each platform has its own vibe, language, and cool kids' club. Think of it like this: you wouldn't wear a ball gown to a beach party, right? Similarly, you wouldn't create TikTok-style content for LinkedIn's boardroom.

We'll explore the unique nuances of popular platforms, from the meme-friendly realms of TikTok to the long-form landscapes of YouTube. Let's break it down.

Instagram: For social media platforms like Instagram and Snapchat, visual content is key. You'll want to focus on creating eye-catching images or videos that grab people's attention as they scroll through their feeds. Use filters, stickers, and emoji's to add personality to your content. It is like the visual storyteller's paradise, where your content is the star of a visually stunning show.

Twitter: Twitter and LinkedIn are the fast-paced, witty coffee shop where your clever one-liners shine. It is the sophisticated networking event where you bring your professional A-game. Understanding these vibes is key to tailoring your content for maximum impact.

Facebook: Facebook is a social network with a large user base of over two billion active users worldwide. Through social sharing, it offers a chance for discreet connection with customers. Mix up your posts with different types of content like photos, videos, and text-based posts. Use storytelling to captivate your audience and make sure to include visuals to grab attention. Keep your posts concise, engage with your audience, and be mindful of timing. Stay positive and respectful in your posts, and analyze your Facebook Insights to adapt your content strategy.

Tiktok: Where brevity is the name of the game, you'll need to get creative with your content. Think short and snappy captions, quick videos, or even GIFs. The goal is to make an impact in a short amount of time. By the end of this section, you'll be the social media multitasker, crafting content that doesn't just fit in but stands out in every digital nook and cranny.

YouTube: You have the opportunity to create longer-form content. This could be in the form of tutorials, vlogs, or even scripted videos. Take advantage of the visual medium by incorporating engaging visuals, graphics, and transitions.

The act of sharing identical content on various social media platforms is also possible. Although, Different platforms may require different types of content to be successful. It's possible that a post that gains popularity on X (Twitter) won't necessarily translate to Facebook and vice versa.

According to Pew Research Center, 69% of American adults utilize social media for various purposes beyond catching up with news and friends or sharing viral videos. Streamlining your postings and taking other steps to improve your brand's social media presence can be of interest to you.

In a nutshell, this chapter emphasizes the essence of knowing your audience, covering aspects like geographic, demographic, and psychographic information.

It stresses that identifying your target audience is pivotal and provides tips on doing so, including analyzing existing followers, researching the niche, understanding competitors, experimenting with content types, and setting goals and core values.

Additionally, the chapter explores the significance of tailoring content for different platforms. It provides insights into the unique characteristics of platforms like Instagram, Twitter, Facebook, TikTok, and YouTube, offering guidance on creating content that aligns with each platform's vibe.

Chapter 3: Crafting Compelling Content

Crafting Compelling Content explores how we can creatively design engaging messages and content that really connect with your audience. Develop a range of techniques – including use of language, characters and the voice we can take on as a speaker – to move our audience.

Weaving in the power of stories we look at how they work, why we are so drawn to them, and the ways in which we can apply this essential human characteristic to create powerful messages.

Crafting compelling content is all about capturing the attention and interest of your audience. It involves creating content that is engaging, informative, and valuable to your viewers.

Here are a few tips to help you craft compelling content:

1. Know Your Audience: Understanding your target audience is key to creating content that resonates with them. Research their interests, needs, and pain points, and tailor your content accordingly.

2. Grab Attention with a Strong Headline: Your headline is the first thing that grabs your audience's attention. Make it catchy, intriguing, and relevant to your content. A compelling headline can make all the difference in getting people to click and read further.

3. Tell a Story: People love stories: Use storytelling techniques to captivate your audience and make your content more relatable. Share personal experiences, anecdotes, or case studies to make your content more engaging and memorable.

4.Use Visuals: Visual elements like images, videos, infographics, and charts can enhance your content and make it more visually appealing. Visuals not only grab attention but also help in conveying information more effectively.

5. Keep it Clear and Concise: Avoid using jargon or complicated language that may confuse your audience. Keep your content simple, clear, and easy to understand. Break it into smaller paragraphs, use bullet points, and highlight key points for better readability.

Remember, crafting compelling content takes practice and experimentation. Don't be afraid to try new formats, styles, and topics to find what works best for your audience. Keep learning, adapting, and refining your content strategy to keep your audience engaged and coming back for more.

Storytelling Techniques

Storytelling is the ancient art of interactive human expression that communicates the narrative and reveals thousands of images and situations while stringing the viewer's imagination.

Storytelling is an art as much as a science. A scientific explanation of our admiration of stories is that it activates the hormone oxytocin that boosts trust and empathy when we hear a moving story. Thus, compelling stories act as motivators and positively influence people's behavior.

Individuals live through stories - everyone loves to settle with friends and listen to their compelling stories. Also, people enjoy thinking about their memories and turning them into interactive narratives.

Why is Storytelling Important for Marketing

As brands face overloaded competition, it is becoming extremely tough to grasp an audience's attention. Customers are exposed to thousands of contents and ads per day, causing a decrease in attention spans.

We all watch content with our eyes but connect with our hearts. The best way to make customers feel like that is by integrating stories into your content marketing strategy.

Yes, that is right! You can use the power of stories to boost your engagement efforts and construct customer relationships. Instead of stating typical features and sales pitchy details, try to produce value-driven content decorated with stories.

Techniques & Examples of Storytelling

AIDA - Attention Interest Desire Action

Attention Interest Desire Action (AIDA) is an effective communication method used in marketing for decades. It outlines a four-step order to deliver message details successfully to your target audience.

Attention - the most decisive part is to gain someone's attention in seconds. There is no time for longer introductions as customers' attention spans are lower.

Interest - As you successfully get viewers' attention, you will face a more complex mission to hold them on your page.

So, the most important thing here is to gain engagement and the viewer's empathy.

Desire - so, your viewers are going nowhere, and now you have to shove how you solve their problems. Try to outline the benefits of making customers' life easier!

Action - the last step is getting your customers to act! No surprise, as each marketing material aims to convert its viewers. So, try to create a sense of urgency.

Tips to consider in story telling:

1.Character Development

Let's dive deep into the captivating world of characters. Picture this: you're crafting a blog post or video, and instead of just throwing information out there, you introduce characters—real or fictional. These characters aren't just placeholders; they're the heartbeats of your narrative. Take the time to build them up with quirks, aspirations, and challenges. Think of them as the protagonists in your content story.

For instance, if you're discussing the journey of a new product, introduce the people behind its creation—the passionate innovators, the challenges they faced, and the triumphs that fueled their determination. By humanizing your content, you create an emotional connection with your audience, making your message not just informative but memorable.

2. Plot Arcs

Now, let's talk about the art of storytelling structure—plot arcs. Imagine your content as a rollercoaster ride. You start with a thrilling climb, introducing your audience to an engaging concept or problem. The middle is where the twists and turns happen—deepening the narrative with insights, conflicts, or unexpected turns. Finally, you descend into the resolution, providing a satisfying conclusion or a call to action.

Consider a case study as an example. Begin by setting the stage, explaining the initial challenge your subject faced. Move into the thick of it—describe the strategies, setbacks, and revelations. Lastly, bring it all home with the resolution, showcasing the positive outcomes or lessons learned. This structure keeps your audience on the edge of their seats, ensuring they stay engaged from start to finish.

3. Emotion Elicitation

Let's get emotional! Think about the last piece of content that really stuck with you. Chances are, it made you feel something—joy, empathy, surprise, or maybe even sadness. Incorporating emotional elements into your content is like adding spice to a dish. It leaves a lasting flavor.

Consider a blog post discussing a community initiative. Share personal anecdotes of individuals impacted by the initiative. Express the joy of success, the empathy for challenges faced, or the surprise of unexpected outcomes. By appealing to emotions, you turn your content into an experience, making it more shareable and relatable.

Building a Unique Personal Brand

The deliberate and strategic process of defining and communicating your unique value proposition is known as personal branding. Even though people have always taken great care to maintain their public personas and reputations, social media and internet search have significantly increased the potential audience for these efforts as well as the risks and benefits that come with them.

Regretfully, despite our desire to believe otherwise, we seldom have total control over our personal brands. "What people say about you when you're not there is what defines your brand" according to Amazon founder Jeff Bezos. It is the culmination of all the associations, expectations, sentiments, and beliefs that people have about you as a whole. Making sure the story being told about you is true, logical, interesting, and unique should be your main concern.

A Seven-Step Process

This approach involves seven steps, each of which informs the others as you move from strategizing to testing to tweaking in response to feedback.

1. Define your purpose.

2. Audit your personal brand equity.

3. Construct your personal narrative.

4. Embody your brand.

5. Communicate your brand story.

6. Socialize your brand.

7. Reevaluate and adjust your brand.

Some few Important tips to also consider:

1. Authenticity

Now, let's shift gears to personal branding. Authenticity is your golden ticket. It's about being unapologetically yourself in a digital world filled with noise. Share the behind-the-scenes moments, the challenges you've overcome, and the lessons you've learned. Your audience wants to connect with a real person, not just a content creator.

Think about a vlog where you share the highs and lows of your creative process. Embrace your quirks, show the real you, and let your audience into your world. Authenticity builds trust, and trust is the foundation of a loyal audience.

2. Consistency

Consistency is the glue that holds your personal brand together. Imagine watching your favorite TV show, and suddenly the characters start acting completely out of character—it's jarring. The same principle applies to your content. Whether it's your blog, social media, or videos, maintain a consistent tone, visual style, and messaging.

Consider a scenario where you're a lifestyle blogger. Your audience expects a certain aesthetic and tone from your content. If you suddenly shift to a drastically different style without explanation, it can confuse and disengage your audience. Consistency, on the other hand, breeds familiarity and strengthens your brand identity.

3. Value Proposition

What's your unique flavor? Your value proposition is what sets you apart in a crowded digital space. Identify your strengths, skills, or perspectives that bring value to your audience. Are you the go-to expert in a niche topic? Do you offer a fresh perspective on common challenges?

Let's say you're a fitness influencer. Your value proposition might be your unique approach to wellness that combines physical health with mental well-being. Clearly communicate this value in your content—whether it's through informative articles, workout videos, or personal anecdotes. When your audience understands what makes you special, they're more likely to stick around for the long haul.

In conclusion, crafting compelling content is an intricate dance between storytelling finesse and personal brand development. By creating characters that resonate, structuring your content with engaging plot arcs, tapping into emotions, and building an authentic personal brand, you elevate your content from mere information to an unforgettable experience. So, go ahead, weave those narratives, showcase your uniqueness, and let your content leave a lasting imprint in the dynamic realm of digital communication.

Chapter 4: Overcoming Camera Shyness

Overcoming Camera Shyness is a transformative journey that individuals embark upon to conquer the fear and anxiety associated with being in front of a camera. Camera shyness, often rooted in the fear of judgment, self-consciousness, or a desire for perfection, can hinder self-expression and prevent individuals from effectively communicating their thoughts and ideas. This chapter explore into the strategies and psychological aspects involved in overcoming camera shyness, emphasizing the importance of authenticity, practice, visualization, and coping mechanisms to build confidence. Through real-life examples and practical tips, we'll explore how individuals can transform their camera shyness into a powerful tool for self-expression and connection.

Let's dive into some 10-steps approach to help you overcome camera shyness:

Step 1: Start Small

Begin by practicing in front of a mirror or recording short videos just for yourself. This allows you to get used to seeing yourself on camera and become more comfortable with your own image.

Step 2: Embrace Your Authenticity

Remember that being yourself is key. Embrace your unique qualities and let your personality shine through. Authenticity is what makes you relatable and connects you with your audience.

Step 3: Prepare and Rehearse

Feeling prepared can boost your confidence. Plan out what you want to say or do in your videos and rehearse beforehand. This will help you feel more at ease and reduce any nervousness.

Step 4: Focus on the Content

Shift your focus from the camera to the message you want to convey. Concentrate on the value you're providing to your audience rather than worrying about how you look or sound.

When you're passionate about your content, it can help you forget about being camera shy.

Step 5: Take it One Step at a Time

Don't rush the process. Start by recording short videos and gradually increase the length as you become more comfortable. Celebrate your progress along the way and don't be too hard on yourself if it takes time to overcome camera shyness.

Step 6: Practice Deep Breathing and Relaxation Techniques

If you feel nervous before hitting the record button, practice deep breathing exercises or other relaxation techniques. This can help calm your nerves and reduce anxiety.

Step 7: Find a Supportive Environment

Surround yourself with supportive and encouraging people who can help boost your confidence. Share your videos with friends or family members who can provide constructive feedback and cheer you on.

Step 8: Embrace Mistakes and Imperfections

Remember that nobody is perfect, and it's okay to make mistakes or have imperfections on camera. Embrace them as part of your journey and learning process. Your audience will appreciate your authenticity and vulnerability.

Step 9: Celebrate Your Progress

Acknowledge and celebrate your achievements along the way. Each time you overcome camera shyness and create a video, give yourself a pat on the back. Recognize that you're growing and improving with each step.

Step 10: Have Fun!

Lastly, don't forget to have fun!

Strategies for Confidence on Camera

The spotlight of a camera can be intimidating, triggering a wave of nervousness and self-doubt. However, transforming camera shyness into confidence is not only achievable but empowering. This section explores strategies that empower individuals to embrace their authentic selves, practice with purpose, and visualize success, ultimately fostering confidence on camera.

Embrace Authenticity

Camera shyness often sneaks in when we worry too much about being perfect. But you know what's perfect? Being you! So, throw perfection out the window, and let your quirks shine. When you're real and authentic, your audience connects with you on a whole new level.

Think about it—vloggers like Casey Neistat or Zoella didn't become stars by pretending to be flawless. They became sensations because they were unapologetically themselves. So, take a deep breath, smile, and let the world see the real, fantastic you.

Practice, Practice, Practice

Now, let's talk practice. It's like learning to ride a bike; the more you do it, the less wobbly you become. Start small—record short videos just for yourself. Talk about your day, share your thoughts, or pretend you're the host of your own show. Practice maintaining eye contact with the camera, and soon, you'll find your groove.

Remember, even the pros weren't born masters. They stumbled through their first takes just like everyone else. So, grab that camera, hit record, and let yourself shine. The more you practice, the more comfortable you'll become in front of the lens.

Visualize Success

Now, let's get our minds in the game. Visualization is like a superhero cape for confidence. Close your eyes and picture yourself confidently delivering your message on camera. Imagine the positive reactions from your audience, the engaging comments, and the feeling of accomplishment. This mental rehearsal rewires your brain, turning anxiety into a confident expectation.

Athletes use visualization to crush it in their sports, and you can apply the same magic to your on-camera game. Your mind is a powerful ally, and when it believes you're a superstar on camera, your performance follows suit.

How to speak with confidence on camera

Undoubtedly, those who are extremely self-assured have an advantage with cameras. We believe it's perfectly acceptable to seek assistance instead of enduring uncomfortable speaking, sweaty palms, and laboured breathing. Here are some quick pointers on projecting confidence when facing a camera

1. Become your own loyal viewer and critic

The simplest way to increase your confidence significantly before going live is probably to practice in front of a mirror. Consider yourself from the perspective of a random onlooker. Recall that only you are aware of all of your imperfections. Not even half are noticed by most people. Furthermore, you can usually forgive the audience much more easily than your inner critic. Therefore, don't be scared to make errors. We all do, after all.

2. Learn and control your body language:

One gesture or particular posture can have a big impact on how you look. Research indicates that we deduce approximately 55% of the information in a conversation through nonverbal cues. That implies that a lot of the time, we use body language to tell whether or not we like someone. It is crucial to take some time to pay attention to the signals that your body sends out because of this. Once your behaviour has been examined, you will be able to project confidence onto the camera with just your body. For example, when a person is confident, they often maintain a relaxed and pulled-back posture.

Psychologists claim that deliberately smiling can increase happiness. The sense of power and confidence can be explained by the same mechanism. Simply give these a try to see the difference for yourself:

- Keep your posture upright.
- Relax your neck muscles.
- Hold your shoulders back.

Keep your body in this position for at least five to ten minutes and you'll feel more comfortable and stronger at the same time. Also, you could try doing yoga right before going live to alleviate unnecessary tension and relax your body.

3.Take care of your health and mood:

Yes, your health and mood, in particular, heavily impact the quality of your content. We cannot stress enough how important this connection is. For instance, you could be tired due to a lack of sleep or dehydration, which in turn will make you less focused and entertaining, thus more self-conscious and nervous.

However, do remember that even if you aren't feeling okay, just try to smile more often and use a bit of humor. A little joke never hurt anyone, as long as it is not racist or sexist. Otherwise, it can ruin your whole career.

4. Look directly into the camera

Just like in real life, maintaining eye contact through the camera lens indicates you are confident. Therefore, don't miss a chance to look your viewers right into their souls. Try to perceive the camera lens as the eye of your good friend. And then, try talking to the camera as if it was your buddy. But, please, don't be creepy! Staring intensely might make your viewers uncomfortable, at the very least, or even leave them wondering if you are all right. It is often recommended to hold eye contact for no more than five seconds.

5. Pay attention to your appearance

What is the first thing you notice when you watch any video of a person? Surely, it's their appearance. The importance of looks simply cannot be underestimated. Not only does a great look attract more viewers, but it can also make you feel more confident, thus maintaining those newcomers. That's why it's in your best interest to make sure you are dressed well, your make-up is neat, and your hairdo is fresh. No one can resist a confident look!

6. Be fully prepared:

What is harder: improvising on stage or reading pre-written jokes aloud? Well, obviously you can become super anxious and lose all your confidence when you don't really know what to talk about. Hence, it is a good idea to write down the main topics you'd like to cover on your video. Ideally, you want to have a full script so you don't ever stumble. But make sure you leave some space for a few improvisations.

7.Use a decent tools:

If you think a good look and an energetic attitude are everything you need to make the audience fall in love with you, unfortunately, it's not true. Some technical factors definitely need to be mentioned.

First of all, every popular content creator knows how much the adequate lighting matters. To put it shortly, good lighting can do wonders! There's a chapter ahead discussing this.

8. Welcome your flaws and mistakes:

Do you remember the very first piece of advice we gave you? We all constantly make mistakes, and that's absolutely okay. However, not all of us learn from our mistakes. Some people are so afraid of failing, they forget it is the most important lesson.

Surprisingly, it is the acceptance of our flaws that allows us to be ourselves and achieve success. Similarly to the impact yoga has on your body, this mindset helps you avoid excessive stress and be natural on camera. Even if you made a mistake in your video, just remember that nobody's perfect.

Dealing with Nervousness and Anxiety

In this fast-paced world, it's not uncommon to feel overwhelmed by nervousness and anxiety. Whether it's before a big presentation, a social gathering, or simply facing new challenges, these emotions can often hinder us from fully embracing life's opportunities. But fear not, because in this chapter, we'll explore practical strategies to help you navigate and overcome nervousness and anxiety.

Ways to Embracing Calmness Amidst Nervousness and Anxiety

Breathing Techniques

When those nerves start doing the cha-cha, it's time for some deep breaths. Seriously, breathe in, breathe out. Deep, slow breaths calm your nervous system and bring you back to center. Before you hit that record button, take a few moments for some diaphragmatic breathing. Inhale the good vibes, let your stomach expand, and exhale the jitters away. It's like a mini spa break for your nerves.

Positive Affirmations

Let's combat those negative thoughts with a dose of positivity. Create your own hype squad with positive affirmations. Remind yourself of your incredible capabilities. Repeat mantras like, "I am confident, articulate, and engaging on camera." It might sound cheesy, but trust me, it works. These affirmations shift your mindset and build a fortress of self-assurance.

Gradual Exposure

No need to dive into the deep end—let's take it one step at a time. Gradual exposure is the name of the game. Start with short, low-pressure videos and slowly turn up the heat. Celebrate the small victories because each successful recording is a step toward conquering camera shyness.

Think of it as leveling up in a video game. You start with the easy levels, gain confidence, and tackle the tougher challenges as you go. Before you know it, you're a camera-shyness conquering champion.

In conclusion, overcoming camera shyness is a journey, not a sprint. Embrace authenticity, practice regularly, visualize success, use calming techniques, shower yourself with positive affirmations, and gradually expose yourself to the camera. With time, dedication, and a sprinkle of self-love, you'll not only overcome camera shyness but discover the joy of sharing your awesome, authentic self with the world. So, grab that camera, hit record, and let the good vibes roll!

Chapter 5: Technical Aspects of Video Creation

Professional outcomes in the field of video creation demand a deep comprehension of the technological factors involved. Every stage is vital to producing an engaging visual experience, from choosing the appropriate tools to becoming an expert in video editing. Welcome to the captivating realm of video production, where creative grace and technological mastery coexist. This chapter will take you on an exciting voyage through the details of necessary equipment, technological marvels, and editing magic to turn your ordinary videos into captivating ones.

Equipment Essentials

The quality of your finished video can vary depending on the equipment you use for shooting. With the proper tools, finishing projects could also be simpler for you. To shoot videos, you'll need some equipment specific to videography, such as your camera and audio connections. You can choose to add additional accessories later on to further elevate the quality of your recordings, such as an extra microphone or tripod or external microphone, you may decide to add later to improve the professionalism of your videos. Below are some few things to look into regarding Equipment Essential.

1. Camera Selection

Choosing the right camera is fundamental to video production. Consider factors such as resolution, frame rate, and low-light performance. High-end DSLRs or mirrorless cameras are popular choices for their versatility and image quality. However, for beginners, modern smartphones can provide impressive results. When choosing the right video camera, consider things like:

Budget: Video cameras come in all different budgets. Consider how much you want to spend on your camera before shopping.

Type of video shooting: Consider the type of video shooting you plan to do, with options like static or stealth. You also want to consider options like high definition or 4K.

Where you publish your videos: How, and where, you plan to publish your videos can help you choose the right camera. You might choose a webcam, action camera or camcorder.

2. Tripod

Tripods are a necessity for recording steady footage. They also make it easier to pan between different views with a smoother transition. When selecting the ideal tripod, take into account factors like:

Durability: If your videography projects take you away from home, you want to choose a tripod that is durable.

Flexibility: You also want to consider how flexible a tripod is. A fluid head tripod allows you to move your camera as needed. You might even choose a slider if you prefer to run and shoot.

Fit: You want a tripod that is made to fit your video camera. Even if you're shooting with your iPhone, there are tripods designed for specific models.

Height: Most tripods can be extended for additional height but do have a limit. Make sure you choose a tripod that is the right height for your subjects.

2. Audio Equipment

Audio quality is often overlooked but is critical for a professional video. Invest in a dedicated microphone, such as a shotgun or lapel mic, to capture clear and crisp sound. Consider using a separate audio recorder for higher quality audio capture. Even if your camera comes with a built-in microphone, a stand-alone one can give you a higher quality of video audio. Having a microphone ensures you capture all necessary sounds when filming. Here are a few microphone types to consider:

Boom pole: A boom pole allows you to capture audio from multiple subjects. It is ideal for larger groups or crowds.

Wireless microphone: A wireless microphone improves audio from your subjects. It is a good option if you don't have someone to hold a boom.

Portable digital: A portable digital audio recorder is an external microphone that you can also use to capture additional sounds.

Shotgun microphone: A shotgun microphone allows you to pinpoint specific audio cues. You can attach it to a boom pole or hold it manually.

Handheld microphone: Handheld microphones are good for run-and-shoot types of videos. They give you more control over movement when you're filming.

3. Lighting Setup

Proper lighting is essential for creating a visually appealing video. Natural light can work wonders, but it's often necessary to use artificial lighting for consistency. Experiment with three-point lighting techniques, ensuring adequate illumination on the subject while minimizing shadows. You can fill in the shadows or draw attention to your focal subject by using a camera light. Additionally helpful as an accessory for interview or documentary filming are lights. Using a light reflector might help you capture better video. You may decide to go with a videography studio lighting kit if you want to shoot the majority of your videos in one place.

4. Software for editing videos

After shooting your movies, you'll require high-quality video editing software. A powerful computer is also required for storing your data and films. The ideal solution for you depends rely on the type of editing you do, as there are many to choose from.

Technical Aspects of Video Creation

Resolution and Frame Rate

Understanding resolution and frame rate is crucial for achieving the desired visual impact. Higher resolutions, such as 4K, provide more detail, while frame rate affects the perceived motion. Balancing these factors depends on the type of content and the viewing platform.

White Balance and Color Grading

Accurate white balance ensures realistic color representation. Experiment with color grading to enhance mood and atmosphere. Professional video editing software allows for precise adjustments, giving you control over the final aesthetic.

Depth of Field

Manipulating depth of field can add cinematic flair to your videos. Achieve a shallow depth of field by using a wide aperture, drawing focus to the subject while blurring the background. This technique is especially effective for interviews and narrative storytelling.

Video Editing Tips

1. Choosing the Right Software

Selecting the appropriate video editing software is crucial. Professional options like Adobe Premiere Pro and Final Cut Pro X offer advanced features and capabilities, while simpler tools like iMovie or DaVinci Resolve are suitable for beginners.

2. Organization and Workflow

Maintain a structured workflow to streamline the editing process. Organize your footage, create a timeline, and label clips appropriately. This ensures efficiency and prevents confusion during the editing phase.

3. Transitions and Effects

Use transitions and effects judiciously to enhance storytelling. Overuse can distract from the narrative, so employ them purposefully to guide the viewer's attention or denote a change in time or location.

4. Audio Editing

Pay careful attention to audio editing. Remove background noise, adjust volume levels, and synchronize audio with video for a polished final product. A well-mixed soundtrack can significantly elevate the overall quality of your video.

5. Exporting and Compression

When exporting your video, choose the appropriate settings for your target platform. Balance file size with quality, considering factors like bit rate and codec. Compression is inevitable, but strive to maintain the highest quality possible.

In conclusion, mastering the technical aspects of video creation involves a combination of equipment knowledge, technical skills, and creative finesse. By understanding the essentials and implementing effective editing techniques, you can elevate your videos to a professional standard, captivating your audience with compelling visuals and engaging storytelling.

Chapter 7: Mastering Effective Communication Skills

The Art of Communication

Understanding the Importance of Effective Communication

The cornerstone of success in both the personal and professional worlds is effective communication. It includes both verbal and nonverbal clues, attentive listening, and the capacity to express ideas concisely. It transcends the simple interchange of words.

Building lasting relationships, settling disputes, and succeeding in a variety of spheres of life all depend on having effective communication abilities. By knowing the requirements, problems, and interests of your target audience, you can better target your messaging and make it more relevant to them. Additionally, it assists you in gaining the credibility and confidence of potential clients, which is essential when making decisions.

The Elements of Effective Communication

Verbal Communication

Clarity and Conciseness: Consider the difference between saying, "I think we should maybe try a different approach" and "I propose we explore a new strategy to address this issue." The latter is clear, concise, and more likely to be understood.

Tone and Pitch: Imagine a manager delivering feedback to an employee. A friendly and encouraging tone can motivate the employee to improve, while a harsh tone might lead to defensiveness and a breakdown in communication.

Speed of Speech: In a classroom setting, a teacher's pace of speech can impact student comprehension. Speaking too quickly might leave students confused, while a slow pace could result in disengagement.

Non-verbal Communication

Body Language: Consider a job interview where the candidate maintains eye contact, sits up straight, and uses appropriate gestures. These non-verbal cues convey confidence and professionalism.

Facial Expression: Think about a conversation where someone discusses a challenging situation with a concerned expression. The facial expression adds emotional depth to the words, emphasizing the seriousness of the matter.

Proximity and Personal Space: In a networking event, being mindful of personal space is essential. Invading someone's personal space may make them uncomfortable, potentially hindering effective communication.

Improving Verbal Communication

Focused Attention: Imagine a counseling session where the counselor actively listens, nodding in agreement and providing verbal affirmations. This attentiveness builds rapport and trust.

Clarification: In a team meeting, a team member might say, "I'm not sure I understood your point about the project timeline. Could you clarify?" This simple act of seeking clarification prevents misunderstandings.

Empathy: Picture a customer service representative empathetically listening to a customer's complaint.

Acknowledging the customer's frustration and expressing empathy can turn a negative experience into a positive one.

Constructive Feedback

Timeliness: Consider a manager providing timely feedback after a successful project completion. This immediate acknowledgment reinforces positive behavior and motivates the team.

Specificity: Contrast vague feedback like "Good job" with specific feedback such as "Your thorough research and attention to detail in the report significantly contributed to our success."

Positivity: Imagine a teacher offering constructive criticism to a student, emphasizing areas for improvement while highlighting the student's strengths. This approach fosters a positive learning environment.

Mastering Non-verbal Communication

Practicing Mindful Body Language

Mirror the Situation: Picture a negotiator adapting their body language to match the formality of a business meeting. This mirroring helps build rapport and a sense of connection.

Cultural Sensitivity: In a multicultural team, being aware of cultural differences in non-verbal communication prevents misunderstandings. For example, maintaining eye contact may be considered respectful in some cultures but disrespectful in others.

Consistency: In a leadership role, maintaining consistency between verbal instructions and non-verbal cues reinforces clarity. Mixed signals can lead to confusion and hinder effective communication.

Polishing Presentation Skills

Voice Modulation: Envision a public speaker modulating their voice to emphasize key points. This variation captures the audience's attention and enhances the overall impact of the message.

Visual Aids: In a business presentation, well-designed visual aids complement spoken words. They can simplify complex information and make the message more memorable.

Confidence: Picture a job interview where a candidate confidently presents their skills and experiences. Confidence instills trust in the interviewer and improves the overall impression.

Handling Q&A Sessions

Anticipate Questions: Before a press conference, a spokesperson might anticipate questions from journalists and prepare responses. This proactive approach ensures they are well-prepared and can address inquiries effectively.

Know Your Material: Imagine a scientist presenting groundbreaking research. A deep understanding of the subject matter allows them to respond confidently and informatively to questions from the audience.

Practice Responses: In a town hall meeting, a political leader might rehearse responses to diverse questions to handle the range of topics effectively. This preparation minimizes the risk of being caught off guard.

During the Q&A Session

Active Listening: Picture a panel discussion where participants actively listen to audience questions before responding. This ensures that the answers are relevant and directly address the concerns raised.

Stay Calm and Composed: In a crisis communication scenario, maintaining composure during a Q&A session is crucial. A composed demeanor reassures the public and instills confidence in the speaker.

Encourage Participation: During a workshop, a facilitator encourages participants to ask questions. This interactive approach fosters engagement and enhances the overall learning experience.

Mastering effective communication skills is an ongoing journey that requires continuous effort and self-reflection. As you integrate these skills into your daily interactions, you'll find that your ability to connect with others, resolve conflicts, and achieve your goals improves significantly. Remember that effective communication is a dynamic skill that adapts to different situations and contexts. By honing your verbal and non-verbal communication skills and adeptly handling Q&A sessions, you position yourself for success in both personal and professional spheres.

Chapter 8: Mastering a Consistent Content Schedule

The Importance of a Consistent Content Schedule

A regular content schedule is crucial in the rapidly changing digital world, where users' attention spans are short and engagement is very competitive. Any effective content strategy is built around a thoughtful and dependable posting schedule, which has several advantages beyond visibility alone.

Learn when you are most productive. To find out, you must first ask yourself.

What hours of the day can I work more intensively?

At what times can I be more energetic?

At what times can I focus more on my work?

Am I a morning or evening person?

To learn these questions, of course, follow yourself. Every time you create content, track what time of day you do it best.

Time Management for Content Creators

Welcome to the world of time management for content creators, where every second may transform your idea into a digital masterpiece and the clock turns into your buddy. Come learn about the tactics, resources, and mentalities that will enable you to approach the world of content creation with accuracy, effectiveness, and a thrilling dash of originality. Prepare to discover the keys to mastering time management and reaching previously unattainable levels of success with your content creation. Now is the time to savour each moment!

Planning and Prioritizing

Content Calendar: A well-organized content calendar is the backbone of consistent content creation. Plan your content in advance, outlining topics, formats, and publication dates. Tools like editorial calendars or project management apps can help streamline this process.

Prioritization: Not all content is created equal. Identify high-priority topics or projects and allocate your time accordingly. Focus on what aligns with your goals and resonates most with your audience.

Batching and Time Blocking

Batching: Group similar tasks together to streamline your workflow. For instance, dedicate specific days or blocks of time to writing, filming, editing, or social media engagement. This minimizes context switching and increases efficiency.

Time Blocking: Assign specific blocks of time to particular tasks. Protect these blocks as you would any other appointment, ensuring dedicated focus on your content creation without constant interruptions.

Balancing Quality and Quantity

Introducing the intricate dance of content creation, in which the need for quantity and the desire of quality clash, leaving creators to balance the two. Every word, every pixel, every second counts in this thrilling world.

Establishing the ideal equilibrium between number and quality is the artistic tightrope walker that distinguishes the remarkable from the great, the prolific from the profound.

Imagine a world in which every content creation is a work of art and the flow is unbroken—a symphony of abundant creativity without sacrificing quality.

Come along on a journey as we reveal the techniques for striking a balance between quantity and quality, as well as how to produce material that both satisfies viewers. appetites for more and captures their hearts.

The Quality Quotient

Understanding Your Audience: Quality content begins with a deep understanding of your audience. Conduct surveys, analyze demographics, and engage with your followers to discern their preferences. Tailor your content to address their needs, desires, and pain points.

Research and Editing: Quality content demands thorough research. Whether you're writing a blog post, creating a video, or recording a podcast, invest time in gathering accurate and relevant information. Furthermore, meticulous editing ensures your content is clear, coherent, and free of errors.

Visual Appeal: In the digital realm, visuals matter. Invest in high-quality images, videos, and graphics. Visual appeal not only captures attention but also enhances the overall user experience. It's the difference between a user scrolling past your content and stopping to engage.

The Quantity Quandary

Consistency Matters: While quality is paramount, consistency is the engine that drives your content strategy. Establish a posting schedule that aligns with your capacity and resources. Whether it's daily, weekly, or monthly, be consistent. It creates a routine for your audience and keeps them engaged.

Repurposing Content: Explore the art of repurposing. A well-received blog post can be transformed into a podcast episode, a series of social media posts, or even an infographic.

Analytics and Feedback: Regularly analyze the performance of your content using tools like Google Analytics or social media insights. Gather feedback from your audience through comments, surveys, or direct messages. This data is gold—it helps you understand what resonates with your audience, guiding your future content strategy.

In the dynamic world of digital content creation, mastering a consistent content schedule, effective time management, and striking the delicate balance between quality and quantity is both an art and a science. As a content creator, your journey involves not only delivering valuable content but also building a lasting relationship with your audience. Remember, it's not just about creating content; it's about creating an experience that resonates, captivates, and endures.

CHAPTER 9: Monetizing Your Content

Congratulations! You've mastered the art of content creation, and now it's time to turn your passion into profit. In this chapter, we'll dive into the exciting world of monetization, exploring various revenue streams and the lucrative realm of collaborations and sponsorships. Using content to generate revenue when consumers view it is known as content monetization. Users may pay you directly or through a third party that uses your content to promote items.

Diverse Revenue Streams

Creating compelling content is just the beginning. To sustain your creative endeavors, it's crucial to diversify your revenue streams. Let's explore some tried-and-true methods:

Ad Revenue:

Leverage platforms like YouTube, where you can monetize your videos through ad revenue. The more views and engagement your content receives, the higher your earnings.

Consider optimizing your content for ads without compromising viewer experience.

Affiliate Marketing:

Join affiliate programs related to your niche. Share products or services you genuinely love and earn a commission for each sale made through your unique affiliate link. Your authenticity builds trust with your audience, making them more likely to make a purchase.

Merchandise Sales:

Design and sell branded merchandise such as T-shirts, mugs, or stickers featuring your logo or catchphrase. Platforms like Teespring and Printful make it easy to create and sell custom products without the hassle of inventory management.

Online Courses and Ebooks:

Share your expertise by creating and selling online courses or ebooks. Platforms like Udemy, Teachable, or Amazon Kindle Direct Publishing can help you reach a global audience eager to learn from your experiences.

Crowdfunding and Donations:

Engage with your community through crowdfunding platforms like Patreon or Ko-fi. Offer exclusive content, perks, or early access to supporters. Some viewers genuinely enjoy supporting creators they love without expecting anything in return.

Sponsored Content

Partner with brands for sponsored content opportunities. Showcase their products or services in your videos, ensuring alignment with your audience's interests. Transparency is key; disclose sponsored content to maintain trust.

Collaborations and Sponsorships

Beyond individual revenue streams, collaborations and sponsorships can open up new avenues for monetization while providing added value to your audience.

Collaborations

Team up with fellow creators for collaborative projects. Whether it's a joint video, podcast episode, or social media campaign, collaborations introduce your content to new audiences. Collaborations also foster a sense of community within your niche.

Brand Partnerships:

Forge partnerships with brands relevant to your content. This could involve sponsored videos, product placements, or brand integrations. Negotiate fair compensation for your time and the value you bring to the brand.

Affiliate Collaborations

Collaborate with companies through affiliate marketing. Negotiate commission rates and explore long-term partnerships. The synergy between your content and their products can create a win-win scenario.

Navigating Sponsorships:

Navigating sponsorships requires finesse and careful consideration. Here are some tips to ensure successful partnerships:

Authenticity First:

Align with brands that resonate authentically with your content and audience. Authenticity builds trust, and your recommendations will carry more weight.

Clear Communication:

Establish clear communication with sponsors. Outline expectations, deliverables, and compensation details in a written agreement. This ensures a smooth collaboration and minimizes misunderstandings.

Audience Alignment:

Prioritize your audience's interests. Sponsorships should enhance, not interrupt, the viewer experience. Ensure that sponsored content seamlessly integrates with your usual style and tone.

Ethical Considerations:

Maintain ethical standards. Be transparent with your audience about sponsored content, and only promote products or services that you genuinely endorse. Trust is your most valuable asset.

Long-Term Relationships:

Build long-term relationships with sponsors. Repeat collaborations with the same brands can lead to more significant opportunities and a stable income stream.

In conclusion, monetizing your content is a journey that involves creativity, strategy, and authenticity. By exploring diverse revenue streams and navigating collaborations and sponsorships with integrity, you can turn your passion into a sustainable and rewarding venture. Get ready to enjoy the fruits of your creative labor!

Conclusion

When it comes to reflecting on your journey, it's important to take a step back and look at the progress you've made. Think about the content you've created, the skills you've developed, and the impact you've had on your audience. Celebrate your successes and acknowledge the challenges you've overcome along the way.

As you reflect on your journey, consider asking yourself some questions. What have been your most memorable content moments? Which projects brought you the most joy and fulfillment? Were there any specific challenges that helped you grow as a content creator? Reflecting on these experiences can help you identify your strengths and areas for growth.

Embracing Reflection

As your journey in content creation unfolds, take time to reflect on the path you've traveled. Consider the evolution of your skills, the impact of your content, and the lessons learned. Reflection serves as a compass, guiding you towards continuous improvement. Notable content creators like Marie Forleo often emphasize the transformative power of self-reflection in honing one's craft. By embracing reflection, you not only appreciate your achievements but also identify areas for growth.

Future Trends in Content Creation

The digital landscape is ever-evolving, and staying abreast of future trends is essential for sustained relevance. Explore emerging technologies such as virtual reality (VR) or augmented reality (AR) that are reshaping content experiences. Creators like Mark Rober, known for integrating innovative technologies into their content, exemplify the potential of staying ahead of the curve.

Diversification of Content Formats

The future of content creation lies in diversification. Beyond traditional mediums, consider exploring emerging formats like interactive content, podcasts, or even immersive experiences. Creators such as Hasan Minhaj showcase how a diverse portfolio of content formats can cater to different audience preferences, ensuring a wider reach.

Sustainability and Social Impact

Increasingly, audiences are gravitating towards content that aligns with values of sustainability and social impact. Creators like Emma Chamberlain actively engage in conversations about sustainability and mental health. Understanding and incorporating socially responsible content practices not only resonate with conscious audiences but also contribute to a positive global impact.

The digital landscape is constantly evolving, and it's important to stay ahead of the curve. One of the biggest trends we're seeing is the rise of video content. Platforms like TikTok and YouTube continue to gain popularity, so exploring video creation can be a great way to engage with your audience. Another trend to keep an eye on is the importance of authenticity and relatability. Audiences are craving genuine connections, so being true to yourself and sharing your unique perspective can help you stand out in a crowded content space.

Lastly, staying up to date with emerging technologies can also be beneficial. From virtual reality to augmented reality, there are endless possibilities for immersive content experiences. Exploring these technologies can open up new avenues for creativity and audience engagement.

Navigating the Uncharted

The conclusion of this journey marks the beginning of new possibilities. Navigating the uncharted waters of content creation requires a blend of reflection, adaptability, and a forward-looking mindset. By embracing both the lessons of the past and the possibilities of the future, you position yourself as a dynamic creator ready to shape the evolving narrative of content creation.

As you close this chapter, consider it not as an endpoint but as a milestone in an ongoing narrative—one that you have the power to shape and redefine. The journey of content creation is not just about the content you produce; it's about the creator you become along the way. Here's to the next chapter in your creative odyssey.

WHAT TO POST

150 FREE TIPS ON VIDEO CONTENT IDEAS ACROSS VARIOUS GENRES TO POST

The process of determining and choosing the most pertinent subjects that would captivate your target audience is known as "content ideation," and it is a word that is frequently used in content marketing. When we refer to information as "engaging," we mean that it should be worthwhile, entertaining, or intriguing enough to be shared. This chapter gives free 150 tips on what to post

1. Vlogs:

1. "A Day in My Life" Vlog

2. Travel Diary Series

3. Behind-the-Scenes of Your Workday

4. Exploring Hidden Gems in Your City

5. Weekend Adventure Vlog

6. Fitness Journey and Progress Updates

7. Cooking and Meal Prep Vlog

8. Road Trip Chronicles

9. Family Day Out Vlog

10. Virtual Travel Experience

2. Educational Content:

11. How-to Tutorials on a Specific Skill

12. Explainer Videos on Science Concepts

13. Language Learning Progress Updates

14. Historical Facts or Fun Trivia

15. DIY Home Improvement Projects

16. Virtual Museum or Art Gallery Tour

17. Book Reviews and Recommendations

18. Math Problem Solving Series

19. Tech Tips and Tricks

20. Coding Challenges and Solutions

3. Entertainment:

21. Comedy Sketch or Parody Video

22. Reaction Video to Trending Content

23. Movie Night Commentary and Reviews

24. Gaming Playthrough and Commentary

25. Talent Show or Skill Showcase

26. Karaoke Night or Lip Sync Battle

27. DIY Magic Tricks Tutorial

28. Escape Room Challenge

29. Unboxing and Reviewing Trending Products

30. Virtual Quiz or Trivia Night

4. Lifestyle and Fashion:

31. Seasonal Fashion Lookbook

32. Thrift Store Haul and Upcycling Projects

33. Makeup and Beauty Tutorials

34. Morning Routine and Self-Care Tips

35. Fashion Trends Discussion and Try-On

36. Hairstyle Transformation Tutorial

37. Wardrobe Declutter and Organization

38. Fitness or Yoga Challenge

39. Sustainable Fashion Haul

40. Day in the Life of a Fashion Enthusiast

5. Tech and Gaming:

41. Gadget Reviews and Unboxings

42. DIY Tech Projects and Hacks

43. PC Building and Setup Guide

44. Game Reviews and Recommendations

45. Esports Tournament Highlights

46. Virtual Reality (VR) Gaming Experience

47. App Reviews and Recommendations

48. Tech Behind-the-Scenes of Your Videos

49. Gaming Setup Tour

50. Coding Livestream or Tutorial

6. Inspirational and Motivational:

51. Personal Growth and Goal Setting

52. Inspirational Quotes and Reflections

53. Share Your Success and Failure Stories

54. Motivational Speech or Talk

55. Mentorship Series with Successful Individuals

56. Discussing Overcoming Challenges

57. Virtual Support Group or Community Gathering

58. Positivity Challenges and Mindfulness Practices

59. Gratitude Journaling Journey

60. Reflecting on Achievements and Milestones

7. Food and Cooking:

61. Cooking Challenge with a Twist

62. Food Taste Test Challenge

63. Virtual Cooking Class with Subscribers

64. Recipe Reviews and Modifications

65. Meal Planning and Grocery Haul

66. Baking or Dessert Making Marathon

67. International Cuisine Exploration

68. Budget-Friendly Meal Prep Ideas

69. Kitchen Hacks and Cooking Tips

70. Cooking Collaboration with Another Creator

8. Challenges and Experiments:

71. 30-Day Challenge Progress Updates

72. Try Not to Laugh Challenge

73. DIY Science Experiments and Demonstrations

74. Mystery Box Challenge

75. Blindfolded Taste Test Challenge

76. Social Media Detox Experience

77. Fitness or Health Challenge

78. Learning a New Instrument Challenge

93. Podcast-style Discussion with Experts

94. Creative Collaboration with Artists

95. Group Challenge or Competition

96. Gaming Session with Friends or Subscribers

97. Cooking or Baking Collaboration

98. Travel Adventure with Other Creators

99. Virtual Panel Discussion on a Trending Topic

100. Community Q&A Session with Subscribers

11. Personal and Storytime:

101. Childhood Memory Sharing Session

102. Relationship Advice and Stories

103. Pet Adoption Story and Updates

104. Personal Finance Tips and Journey

105. Discussing Personal Cultural Heritage

106. Day in the Life of a Student or Professional

107. Reflecting on Family Traditions

108. Personal Travel Mishaps and Adventures

109. Virtual Family Reunion or Gathering

110. Memory Lane: Looking Back at Old Photos

12. Environmental and Sustainable Living:

111. Zero-Waste Lifestyle Tips and Hacks

112. Sustainable Fashion and Shopping Tips

113. Eco-friendly DIY Projects

114. Documenting a Day of Eco-Friendly Choices

115. Thrift Store or Vintage Shopping Haul

116. Gardening Tips and Plant Care

117. Upcycling and Repurposing Old Items

118. Virtual Beach or Park Cleanup

119. Exploring Local Farmer's Markets

120. Minimalist Living Room Makeover

13. Hobbies and Creativity:

121. Art and Craft Time-Lapse

137. Science Experiments with Everyday Items

138. Exploring Space and Astronomy

139. Virtual Tour of a Tech Innovation Center

140. Robotics Project Build and Showcase

15. Relationship and Social:

141. Virtual Date Night Ideas

142. Anniversary Celebration Vlog

143. Long-Distance Relationship Tips

144. Friendship Appreciation Day

145. Relationship Tag or Challenge

146. Group Online Game Night

147. Virtual Hangout Session with Friends

148. Meeting Subscribers in Virtual Space

149. Discussing Social Issues and Awareness

150. Virtual Book Club Meeting

Feel free to mix and match these ideas, adapt them to your style, and let your creativity flow!